The
Plath
Cabinet

Catherine Bowman

Four Way Books
Tribeca

Editorial Office
Four Way Books
POB 535, Village Station
New York, NY 10014
www.fourwaybooks.com

Library of Congress Cataloging-in-Publication Data

Bowman, Catherine.
  The Plath cabinet / Catherine Bowman.
    p. cm.
  ISBN 978-1-884800-86-3 (pbk. : alk. paper)
  1. Plath, Sylvia--Poetry. I. Title.
  PS3552.O87555P63 2009
  811'.54--dc22

                          2008043326

This book is manufactured in the United States of America and printed on acid-free paper.

Four Way Books is a not-for-profit literary press. We are grateful for the assistance we receive from individual donors, public arts agencies, and private foundations.

This publication is made possible with public funds from the New York State Council on the Arts, a state agency.

State of the Arts

NYSCA

Distributed by University Press of New England
One Court Street, Lebanon, NH 03766

[clmp]
We are a proud member of the Council of Literary Magazines and Presses.

Table of Contents

This is a case without a body.

—Sylvia Plath, "The Detective"

Sylvia's Mouths

That mouth made to do violence on,
the straight mouth, mouth's instant flare,
cave-mouth, mouth skewered on a groan,
Mother, you are the one mouth, all-mouth
licks, frog-mouth, fish-mouth. I'll fly
through the candle's mouth, mouth opens
clean as a cat's. Mouth-hole or eye-hole,
I draw on the old mouth, mouth full of pearls,
his mouth's raw wound, cupped quick to mouth,
mouth-plugs, mouth-hole crying their locations,
gold mouths cry, gleaming with mouths of corpses.
A garden of mouthings, I am all mouth.

Sylvia's Bestiary

Attractive cold war wives, graceful and aplacental—
bread-and-butter letters hand-delivered after

cocktail hour—baffle babies' ears with tails.
Disquieting muses, the nursery sluts prepare cake in silence:

easter eels, elm ticklers, embouchure for dolls. Engrailed
fish-girls, ice-boxed to the waist in scale, anticipate

glassfuls in the green grove, stars, bluets,
honeybees and huge male poets.

Ink incubators churn out criminal
jackdaws, footlings, ring fingers,

kiosks of bites on the neck, umbilicals.
Lonely goats, plumed heirlooms, and sadistic

monks brood over
nests for black boots.

Oyster fork, fish fork in flight:
pretend birds suck poppies in July.

Quick now, sweep up the tracks left on the breasts, evidence.
Rabbit masks

stitched by queer aunts.
Tethered by *ich,*

upside down from trees
virgins sway, draft ointments,

weep into hand mirrors, calculate
xineohp × phoenix.

Yew widows stateside douse Yardley, practice the art of
zootechny.

Sylvia's Bed

Bigger than a bee box. Smaller than the stone
cold sea off Sand Flat Cemetery. Bigger than the pump
stopper in the French cut fleur-de-lis. Softer than the earthen tone
of one Welsh tenor. Harder than the ump's
after-game rounder. Black black blacker
than oblivion unopposed. White
as a bleached-out field of cornflower
sequins scoured while squinting into the Wellfleet sun. All that lacks
is near or farther, higher and lower. Quieter than the flow
of the underground river. Louder than gossip
hives. Smaller than Daddy.
Bigger than a moon christened
and made new, ready for five heavens, add
or subtract a few. Wider than a Christ
boat, overturned at the Isle of Tombs. Place to sip
sherry, ice-skate wearing only a crown
across a regal four-poster. Narrower than a mountain
valley filled with mythology's debris. Long as a crow's
questionnaire. Milkier than a milky
cloud basket. Here there be
dragons and every other ilk
of instrument to invent in the tongue's bed.

Sylvia's Honey

The year we first tasted Sylvia's honey. Dipped our fingers deep into the page, into the raw and unfiltered, the highly spun. That year and forever after. The golden bough that tricked us into the underworld.

That was the year we dubbed ourselves Dumb Bitches. Dee-Bees. Joy and I sitting in Pancho's All You Can Eat Mexican Buffet on the west side of San Antonio, just down the road from Randy's Rodeo, where a mob of Texas shit-kicker teens had made headlines for hurling Lone Star longnecks at the Sex Pistols.

A man two booths away raging at the woman across from him.
—Shut the fuck up, you worthless dumb bitch cunt.

Joy looked at me and said:
—Hey dumb bitch, pass the salsa.

D.B., engraved with ancient glittering sharks' teeth on our mistitled upside-down Texas crowns. And Sylvia Plath, our martyred honey goddess, our Queen D.B. In a town where you could find the Virgin of Guadalupe tattooed across a man's back, Our Lady of Sylvia emblazoned into our feet and tongues.

So many of our smart brilliant friends were in trouble. Tonya gang-raped at thirteen, now drugged and locked in at Santa Rosa Hospital; Sharon, hiding naked on Christmas Eve behind a car wash, her doctor husband searching for her with army-issue flashlight and shotgun. Valerie, stabbed to death in broad daylight while jogging with her baby. A rage suppressed comes soaring and creeping out in ugly ways.

※

That year Joy and I were studying politics and philosophy at St. Mary's. Doc Crane, an Adlai liberal who loved boys from the border, told us stories about Yahoos and morals, the old dirty days of Texas politics, mystification, how deals were made over margaritas at Ma Crosby's down in Ciudad Acuña. The different ways a man and a vote could be bought and sold. After class, Joy delivered a luminous explanation of Marx and Habermas. My little brother looking up from the table.

—Man she really laid that smooth. Go for it like a big dog.

O pardon the one who knocks for pardon at your gate,
father—your hound-bitch, daughter, friend.

Big dogs. Dumb Bitches.

Dirty girl,
Thumb stump.

I was going to school, waitressing at the Bijou, hanging out, listening hard, Clifford Scott at the Sugar Shack, the mariachis at the Esquire after hours. I had an apartment above two ancient sisters who thought I was possessed by the devil and brewed smelly comfrey teas for me to clear up my complexion. They gave me an old pair of silver high heels. Poet and activist Ricardo Sánchez asked me to read my poems at his bookstore, Paperbacks y Más. My philosophy professor gave me a B on my Urban Renewal paper, telling me later at a party I would look good nude on a haystack. That was cool, he was taking me seriously as a poet. I wrote my final in rhymed couplets.

One night at the Broadway 50/50 we played the jukebox. Joy grabbed my arm.

—Come on, D.B., let's dance.

We knew that at this longitude and latitude and under this light, we were both supremely D.B., and we danced and laughed. Her words became us. A honey that hurt. That healed. That we couldn't stop wanting. That would bear us out. Sylvia's clove-orange honey. *The bees are flying. They taste the spring.*

Sylvia's Stove

Suddenly, with a gust, the door
blew shut, leaving her locked out,
her keys in the empty flat.
Arriving in London in January subzero
she found the electricity still
disconnected and the stove
uninstalled. When the gas boys arrived,
they scaled the roof, budging
a bracket on a window, sliding in,
then kindly installing the stove
using only candlelight.

Viola Practice, 1945

Cut snowflakes, river's eve outlined in ash, viola practice.
On New Year's, Mother alone sits with midnight—
Lone Ranger on the radio. Viola.
She can play two notes now with her fingers.

On New Year's Day, Mother alone sips on midnight.
Her shoes too tight. She practices viola,
over and over two notes now with her fingers.
Reprimanded, why didn't you dust under the principal's desk?

She practices the shape of viola. Both shoes too tight.
While the ink blots, she drinks Arlene's cream—
reprimanded, dust all over the principal's desk,
she paints a border of valentines and presidential hatchets.

The ink blots, she drinks Arlene's cream,
arranges a chemistry lab in the bough of an apple tree,
paints valentines and presidential hatchets,
cuts rivers, outlines her ash blue in viola, practices snowflakes.

Paper Dolls: Toy Theater

Other things on paper: death certificates, gum wrappers, lunacy papers, razor-blade wrappers, receipts, folk recipes, telephone cards, perfume cards, clippings. Kept in a toy trunk, little costumes with transportable bodies for a toy theater.

Paper Dolls: Melon Dress

Her melon dress, her mouth-me dress, her mud-mattress dress, a green bric-a-brac suitcase of bird calls, Tyrolean pie lattice from the waist up, from the waist down topsy-turvy melon slices on a dirndl meringue glacée. A solstice of cream. A see-saw dress. A ding-dong bell. The melon maiden is melon laden, busy learning tongue twisters, practicing the art of inventing music from mock apple and mock rainbow. Melons fall from the sky. O mottled rind and edible flesh—the earth and all the earth's emanations: bull's blood and the musk from the whale's blowhole. In the garden, she paints each slice a shade of lipstick. "Your spy-gown," the great horned owl says to her. "Believe in angels," he whispers, and leads her to the melonry.

Sylvia's Sled

Through the leafless cherry trees,
past two black houses skewed, tilting inward,

in merriment and savagery. Sylvia squints into the light,
snow smudged, Warren on her back, poised ready to fly

down the hill fast, faster: the weight of her brother,
little explorers across a tundra, Winthrop's backwoods,

an excavation through trees encased in ice glass.
Not yet wild or old enough to whisper,

the marriage was not a happy one.
Two pilots with no navigational skills. The sled an ark,

every variation of two as Venus moves
from upper world to shaft, their celestial canoe

scoring a sea of milkfish and sleeping tubers. The sled blades
etch a cosmogram in snow-patterned cells of beehive.

Then household hearth for after-elixir. All possibility,
they choose to join, not capture a pirate's nightbird fleet.

Eternal Blackout

Clouds gone, trees too, no feminine nature,
only oblivion, no conviction of oblivion, no
Mrs. Hughes or Mr. Joyce. No sex, no
parents to distrust. No pies, no
leaves of silk gowns. No Perry Norton. No
east or west wind, dances,
totes, equinox ballets. No baby, dust and black
earrings, then heaven can open.

Paradise, 1956

Lifted wings, talon-magic,
white peonies—four full
quarts of milk—swift now

through luminous willows fallow
with loss, sun-stained
sherry and orange poinsettia

curtains—late afternoon nap
with Teddy. A gorgeous birthday feast—
smoked pheasant, salmon, Chablis.

Writing a dream poem
on the wing of a seabird
white. Scrubbing the enamel sink.

Mornings by the fire—
Tarot and hot milk.
Talking with the dead.

Laundromat, butcher—heavy rains—
his great pushing hands.
Blue moon mist—

fish-in-milk—stiff cider.
Red love in a good hotel
called Paradise.

Paper Dolls: Mermaid Gown

A dripped-on mermaid gown, glistening scales with matching fur. A cobra umbilical bandeau lined with mother-of-pearl. Hybrid of leopard and aquatic night cat, she is going to Santiago de Cuba with Lorca in the back of a black water car.

Sylvia's Second Marriage

Back at the casita, the new Mrs.
Ricky Ricardo hides her purchases
and plots screwball revenge,

disguising herself not as a hot dog salesman
but, again, as a tortured genius.
Bonking her head
on the top of the oven

when Ricky makes his entrance,
baton and roses in hand, singing
thanks to the god of crossroads,
saying, *Sylvia, you got some 'splainin' to do.*

❧

Mayhem ensues as usual
when Mr. and Mrs. Ricardo
arrive at Club Babalu:

she in a gown, white
and wrapped tight as a top-
secret White House memo
erased, hair bottle-red, aflame,

he hot behind the congas,
they reenact vows in tight hard
gutturals. Rhumba couplets
drive the crowd wild.

❧

An orange moon rises—
above Havana's seawall,
an avenue named for
Mr. and Mrs. Song.

Wedding Invitation I

Mr. and Mrs. Smile of Iceboxes
request the pleasure of your
Eelish Delvings
at the wedding reception
of their Bent-backed Atlas
and
Mr. Tongue of Wood
at Horny Pot o'clock in the afternoon
Lever of His Wet Dreams
Weedy Greens, Vermont

Paper Dolls: Clover Coronation Gown

A spring ballgown. Two matching wigs, one white and one blue. Is she etched out of a field of clover in her four-leaf clover gown? Or is she clover queen, covered in clover for the clover bees? The gown, a luscious game board cut from a field of green. Her bee-stitched belt to hang on a favorite fruit tree and swing. Everyone knows the serpent will not touch the shamrock. Her sport, sustenance: disguise.

Picnic at Gobbledygoo

Under a Plath tree,
bring me a fresh-squeezed
serenade. Bring me a cup-o'-pure
under the Plath tree.

Take me down Sylvia's path
for windswept repast, engrossed
over arc and under aorta,
do not trespass or preen,

turn me left at blameless, right me
at sneeze. On the Plath grass wild
with wild onions' plethora
make me sneeze,

bitch. Make me pasture, lathered
across this trespass.
Jelly-roll my options,
make me telepathic

on all fours, paroled. Tie me
to that Plath tree, fill me ample,
make me bleed plateau. *Psst, Quiet now,*
Plath me in half, grammaticized.

Slow me for a quick back flip
at half screw the moon, the tiny hour's
hiccup, now fast, fast, faster—
beware the toothy pitter-patter, the seismic glee

of Plath patrol. Make me numb,
a featured dish—platinum blown.
Play girl. Grill. Grrr...
Sauerkraut. Sauce.

Sylvia's Snakecharmer

1.

They keep your hair here under lock and key
at the rare books library. Poets and scholars arrive in town,
giggle nervously and say oh how very creepy

but still ask to see your braid, and when no one
is looking touch it. I wonder how much
they paid you for your hair? And did you spend

the money on practicalities, or on a steak
with Ted? Now with a strand or two in a test tube
we could reproduce 1000 Sylvia Plaths. On a velvet settee

in your Boston suite, 61 Willow Street,
you manufacture a man that is all snake.
I grew up in the desert with snake-men too.

Around a deep desert well we sang to diamondbacks,
not knowing that our mouths were snake mouths.
He licks the windowpane. Reveals in song the snake

of everything. *The snake-warp, snake-weft*
of skin. Winter trees. Guts. Snowy rivers. Stars—
the bridge between a man and a woman.

2.

Say snake sixteen
times, put it

in a cup,
throw it across
the page like dice.

Say snake
sixteen times.

Put it in a cup,
throw it
across the page
like dice.

Say snake sixteen times,
put it in
a cup, throw it—

across the
page like dice.

The Sylvia Convention: Flower Rooms

Sylvias as Amaryllis aproned
whip up cakes, creams, chicken livers.
Sylvias as fields of Baby's Breath practice
interviews for the BBC. Calla Lily
Sylvias change nappies, type Ted's poems, hope
for enough money to hire a nanny,
wake at 5 writing the best poems of their life.
Daisy Sylvias jump on trampolines.
Sylvias as Evening Primrose conference
with Pan in his suite. Feverfew Sylvias
and Grape Hyacinth Sylvias stir
cauldrons of snakes, ace exams,
take Mademoiselle handwriting analysis.
Now Sylvias are Iris, svelte and stylish,
throwing back cocktails as they flirt wildly
with handsome, award-winning poets.
Jersey Rose Sylvias bathe on the Jersey shore.
King's-spear Sylvias attend seminars
on torture and metaphor. Love-lies-bleeding
Sylvias scrub the kitchen floor, write
letters home to mother. Marigold Sylvias,
Nightshade Sylvias against the garden walls
practice folding and unfolding themselves.
Orchid Sylvias dangle from red
and black balloons. Periwinkle
Sylvias, Queen-Anne's-lace Sylvias,
Red Rose Sylvias look for all things dark:
Sylvia as Salvia. Private. No one allowed.
Thistle Sylvias, Ulster Mary Sylvias, Violet and

Windflower Sylvias, Sylvias as Xeranthemum,
Yarrow, and Zinnia, hundreds and hundreds
gather, write poems like lightning, each one
quicker than the last: an *irresistible blaze.*

Last Wishes, 1963

Someday she would like a pony
for Frieda. To rebuild the cottage,
to have a live-in nanny and lead
a freer life. She will try to go
to Ireland to purge herself
of this awful experience.
She wants blue to be her
new color, wants midnight,
not aqua. She wants to apply
for a Guggenheim, use her birthday check
on a rose-quartz tweed suit. She wants

some of those hair grips. Copper
or wood, a curved oval,
with a pike through the back,
for braids or a crown.
She hopes Frieda and Nick
learn horseback riding very young.
She longs for a second-hand piano,
she has a great yearning to practice
the piano again—she wants to learn
riding, straight riding, no jumping
or hopping or skipping—

she would like nothing
better than to hit it lucky,
to take a London flat. She wants
to learn to milk the TT-tested
Irish cows. She'll have a salon in London,
get her brain back and practice

to write herself out of this hole.
I know just what I want
and I want to do it. She wants time
to breathe, the sun and sea,
to recover her flesh.

Stars that year—

Star fields of 1000 and 1000
daffodils, bees crawling through his hair,
a photo of a lady shooting a jaguar:
the barrelhead of her rifle, the tiny beginnings
of strawberries when she shuts her eyes.
Stars stuck all over, bright stupid confetti—
a Dutch tea set in the cranny. The stitching
from an old hand-wound sewing machine.
Beads for Frieda. A wind-up doll.

Things to Do, 1944

Learn proper posture, study planets, get lowest
grade on test (shh! don't breathe a word), work
on World War notebooks, go through torture
of bath and hair braiding, start a tongue-twister club,
paint an arched-back mermaid, proclaim desire
to be God, make cream puffs in foods class,
learn how Nature protects her animals.

Paper Dolls: Skating Skirt

She races across the ice oval in a crimson ice-skating skirt, long tapered legs the color of grade school chapstick. Ice-skate boots, tapered, almost nonexistent: she seems not to have feet at all, only two white foot points. Trees made of elaborate candles and glass deer miniatures surround her: a red bird, eiderdowned with an ermine ruffle, red armored with a downy interior. A baptismal ice tong. Etiquette instrument for the Christmas feast. Fox girl in the ice kitchen. The choice cut that's in the oval. The question is whether to skate or fly.

Wedding Invitation II

Mrs. S. Swallow It All
and Mr. A. Umbilicus of the Sun
announce the Dog-head, Devourer of their daughter
Endless Glitter
to
Mr. Tell Me My Name
on Sleepdrunk, the twenty-eighth of Marrowy Tunnels
Crocodile of Small Girls Country Club
Hairy Spirit, Illinois

The Plath Candy Company

Oils, molds, sucker sticks,
cauldrons of moon words,
vats for vowelettes. She tosses

cat dice across rose pink
bedsheets, sprinkles
Yaddo dust on dirty pie belly.

This is the midnight series. Broken candy
doll eyes stare from a blue barrel,
a glitter-hive of crystallized eyes,

iridescence to donate to the doll hospital.
Plithy, plathy, plither-plother,
sing the wren-winged workers

as they stretch and pull scorpion
suckers, slut wiggles, variegated
elbow-on-tables and boy things.

The giant mixer churns, glitter-ale
ratcheted up to the seventh—
women-in-love, women-in-love—

thrice hand-dipped, thrice-distilled
in essence of animal God, truffled
samplers cool on the cooling rack,

asterisks for resurrection: the double,
the devil-bird, the sleepwalker.
A pomade of misanthropic angel pop awaits

shaping cutters, dipping forks,
thermometers. Built on the ruins
of an assassin's den and a packing house,

the slate floor weft with what was once
feral. In the sugar room
all that is terrifying becomes candy:

Day-Glo daddy saddles,
Bluebeard keys, chocolate ovens,
steam cook to the hard crack stage.

A black candy train
chuffs on its candy track.
And honey. And honey. And honey.

Diary Starts, 1943

Dear sweet diary, Today is the day of my
Oh hum drum diary, Some old deep dark
Little diary, Mother has bought me
Diary, dear, How I waste
Sad little diary, Something prompts
Dear diary, What possesses me
Dear delectable diary, Look how my fountain

Paper Dolls: Gold Hostess Frock with Top Hat

Top hat, double-D breasts, a long-sleeved lion tamer's waistcoat, leather choker. A leather apron drafted from fairy-tale leftovers. A golden petticoat extracted from sunburst. She'll wear this tonight at the pleasantest of all social occasions, the little dinner. The beasting will begin at half past eight. Strawberries should be impaled on a fork. Tangerines, stripped of their skins, segmented and eaten with the fingers. A handled cup is held with the thumb just above the support grip; the little finger follows the curve. Lift her apron up and it's all lion radiance. After supper, a parlor game, the adults-only lion roar.

Things to Do, 1951

Devour Perry fireside over apple spice pie.
Gobble up Eric and his red MG,
all in one piece on a wide stretch

of Wellfleet beach. Wolf down
Mike alone at the egg farm, be wolfed
back by Pete, as is his habit.

Gorge whole on Jim. Hallelujah!
Spoon Mike up from the jewel box. Amble home,
footsore after balancing platters

for drunk sacramentarians, those lofty specialists
in the spirits. All for just a fishskin of silvers.
Dance in the kitchen with a masculine

caesura. Devise a system for sugar bowl
arrangement, for the engagement of sighs,
for long luxurious kisses and still have the scrub

and polish of crinoline. Mount artwork,
sunset series turned into napkins quite covered.
Remove all nouns verbs and adjectives and replace

with knife, spoon, and fork. Shop, wash
hair in lemon. Storm the confessional with Charles
after making Martin covenant. Eat like a horse,

Howard and his stable of horses
after collecting sunstars, hand in hand,
at the Sand Flats cemetery. Stuff myself with Frank

and his knowledge of hypnosis and Hungarian
under rain-hiss, like a belly-god, a cormorant.
How we sing unction in unison—

Summer Dates

She would rather practice the slice
and drop of his full swing volley,
his perfect racket pitch

than lunch with a sideways
glance, those greens that made her
remember a biology

lesson on how we're made
almost all of water. Rather drink in
hulking slow kisses under big stars,

agog with a jagged rock,
than a slow hotel burn
with a broad-shouldered cardigan,

rather decipher immutable couplets
from his chalice. Rather quicken
the dealer's hands leading her

into the cardia of cave spiral
than gallivant with the long legs
of a Kentucky bluegrass. How the lanterns

made fish patterns on the chapel wall
as they square-danced, cardboard wings
tied to their feet—rather the oblique angel

beckoning from the breakwater's
crevice. Rather marvel over a glinty redhead's
rope tricks, lassoes and stunts,

his tongue twisters, than buccaneer
the races with a handsome stormy sky,
the whirling roar, the smell of exhaust.

From the terrace, a sprinkler-wet lawn,
a paintbrush over lily pads, weeping willows,
the soft glow of his Victrola—

rather slip, afterwards, down the raspberry path,
whistling, this trumpet's expert lips.
At last to kiss him in the red canyon.

Rather drive all the narrow back roads
with a husky voice, leave her
loafers near the gear shift, than guzzle

ale on the porch
with a well-known
pair of blue shorts.

Sylvia's Photo Album

(arranged chronologically)

Front view, sitting at slight angle.
Front view, wearing string of pearls.
Front view, close-up.
Front view, wearing white sweater.
Front view, looking to left.
Front view, looking down and to right.
Front view, big smile.
Front view, sitting at angle, bare shoulders.
Side view, looking at crystal ball held above head.
Holding crystal ball in front of face.
Plath and brother Warren, made into Christmas card.
Plath in one-piece bathing suit.
Plath and Ted Hughes in Paris.
Plath in nurse outfit.
Plath models the blue fabrics.
Plath in boat with fish at Yellowstone.
Plath and children Frieda and Nick.
Plath. Head only; mounted on cardboard.
Woods and field with river.

Sylvia's Passport

Permitted to land
as a student—little green book,

the same slim green as a Faber
and Faber first volume,
a saddle, hauls her...a little green fellow...

her greeny green. Passported, she hunts
for her vessel, a watery reflection,
a crossing. She is all vessel now—
all mouth, inside a mouth.

She is a Jonah. *Milk van.* A milk vat.

The heel steps down,
movement becomes morphine,
from the metal rung.

She's on official business.
She's got deportment
of states. Her hair in place—
a penalty for private use—so use
your phone voice, please.
She is cloud enfranchised. Filled
with cloud. Compart-
mentalized, she's filed.
An alphabetical cloud file.
She's up to her suit—high up—
registered. Paid her dues.

She's got surveillance training
from the gods. She can decode
clouds, vestibules—wrapped as she is
in capsule, in vessel. She is crossing:
The clouds are a marriage dress.

Pass the port portside.
Your liquors seep to me,
in this glass capsule.
She is a benefit, an extract:
she is tree-made. A deep grafting—
liquors seep up from
a Plathian rain forest—
she is craving the tumult
of ocean and rave. She is
a whale or inside a whale
(this may sound fishy to you).
Double-toothed torn margin,
whale bone and leaf bone,
a heavy elixir and conifer cache.
And this is when she goes all domestic.
This is her backup tool. The feather duster
trees. It's all perspective.

The clouds: *a marriage dress.* She had
no idea what she was being dressed
for, wrapped in words
that secreted heresy and orthodoxy
over the frozen subsoil,
the leaching soil—towline
for the vessel, the vehicle. The clouds
began addressing her,
undressing her: privateer bathed in
cloud action—froth after God froth
came, she was crossing over
the world accumulation
below her, from this point—
cloud families made her
snowy, made her an ice rag,
fealty, an aggregate of slide.

She is No. 796203. She is in
sequence. The clouds
a marriage dress—sequined—blunt—
I would admire the gravity of it—
she and her passport, rough-
shorn, unbound, her new set
of Samsonites lined with oasis
and sandpapered, kettle stitched,
organdy joints, she-port and extra thread.
She takes her passport out of an envelope
and unveils its sleek green
upholstery. There is no eye
on the binder, but it
winks at her.

And we are taking off—
look at her,
she is flight

stiffened.
Water seeps into this craft,
an ink. She is an ink machine.

❧

Signed June 29, 1955—
under a red sun. Visa
stamps in candy-color
ink blocks, the kind we're taught
to make things from.
Ted is dead. The Seal of the State
Department. Gold stamped,
two bundles in each talon,
eagle spread.

࿐

Now it is all fog-denial:
pages 16-32, blank visa pages.
How clean pain is—

as are all those departures—
so too Jonah's dream of
a whale. Heartache.

She did not bite an apple,
she bit a whale and
the world turned to

blood. Clouds do nothing
for her now. Take her passport in
your hands.

Sweet angel, dice, tool.
This is a gambler's trade. You know,
she is a bit of a liar.

The veins of the spine, the fine
fine binding—O
ruby—she is in you.

She is always there
on the border, at the edge—
the water's pitch, the Icelandic
scratch, a line through Plath,
a borderline—
thirsty with nothing
but this stash of words:
she walks, all edge,
a document. Dry on your
kingdom's border.

Spy? A traitor?
By taking an oath,
nation status may be lost,
she may lose much.
She wants kingdom. To be bordered.
It's a control issue. A passport
has been issued. Will you not
grant her sovereignty?
Her passport closing in
on the United Kingdom.
She is thirsty
but cannot speak of hunger
on his kingdom's border.

∂ॐ

Her white leather purse where she kept it—
ordered it—next to a lipstick—
a place for renewals, restrictions, amendments—
dark wood, dark water—her green doorstep.
Clouds pass and dispense;
money makes a lovely decoration
when stacked.
Leaves blowing hard,
sharp charms on a bracelet,
visa stamps. How she opens up.
That is what a passport is for.
That is the plan. How the landscape becomes her
registered official business.
To cross the border,
the garden where he lurks
and where he tends—it wasn't an apple—
her passport, the green deep
in her pocket, she's got green
here, because it has always been about the ferryman.

Sylvia's Ritual

Brunching on liver and bacon and then a quick
morning dive down to the underworld
where the oracle takes you on a ferry ride,
reads the future in a change of nappies.
Then to compose from a whistling deck
of smooth sumac. To wash toilets in the twilight,
then under a full moon you batter
a magic chalice with suds: the altar
lights lemon slices on a celery platter: the Eucharistic
vestments a lyrical apron as you iron skirts and slacks
in the eastward position. Each bud in the vase
arranged, a cotillion of Christs. The red roses
pulse with ecstasy as you pick up Farex, brand meats,
stamps at the post office, wafers at the chemist.

Dimensions

Baby crib	The interior is 52 inches long and 28 inches wide.
Oven	26.5 inches wide, 22.5 inches deep, 13.5 inches high.
Typewriter	11 inches wide by 3.26 inches high. Total weight 11 pounds.
Paper	8 inches wide by 11 inches high. The official size determined in 1921 by the Committee on the Simplification of Paper Sizes appointed by the Bureau of Standards as part of the program for the Elimination of Waste in Industry.

Paper Dolls: Three Black Skirts

Three black skirts. Three black rooks. Three black tulips. The pupils widen and widen until all is raw ink. Now it is nighttime—zero brilliance—the dark half-world, the lower world, the other hemisphere. Three black glass blown lamps for the casino. Place your bets for the blackjack's ace. Three black skirts in eight black shades: grotto lung, torch god, urge, uh, French noon, egg foo, yuletide, and her brother's masculine typewriter. Mathematical skirts. They are clocks. Little obsidian mountains, tick-tocks, there's no one on top. Three black skirts! Full and tight as a train whistle. Dilation distilled, only train tunnels here. Black dove annunciation. Three glass black bells. Good luck comes in threes. Three times the black dog swims in a circle. Conversational volcano jars. Three black skirts! Flared heaviness just right for a belt. Lady of the house, she must invent only black flowers, tend her black hens and their precious black eggs. She keeps the floors polished and the hearts fattened in the state room. The sea breaks in—pick a skirt, any skirt: number one, number two, or number three. And in the evening him—pink paws—a lick of milk along a royal highway. Now, let's paint mouths.

Things to Do, 1953

See Gordy. Marty. *Vanity Fair* tea,
Golden Bough subcommittee, Holy Grail settee,
New Yorker tease, *Vogue* tea, *Atlantic* rejectee.
Write T, shorthand Ts, *Mademoiselle* teas,
shock T., Marty? Tennis party.

The Martyrdom of Sylvia Plath

The heart and guts hang hooked,
chaste as snow. Cruel nettles
sting her ankles raw.

She stands burning,
retching into bright orange
basins. Thorned hands

winnowed by angles,
laid waste and unshriven,
desire only God. Gut feasting,

the knot of worms, flies watch,
prove that flesh is real, flawed
earth-flesh, charred and ravened,

body's bait. Flayed,
she treks his mouth's wound, a strict mask.
She wears a wooden girdle

pocked by rook-claw. A spike-
studded belt, drawn tight
around her head stitched bald. Knotweed:

her feet stuck under the meanest table.
She is flea-ridden, drinking vinegar, nerves
to the rack, amorous arrows twined

to her hard limbs. O bent bow of thorns,
her pin-stitched skin, dry tongue's guilt. In his fist,
chaste as snow, engraved in ice, window of my hurt.

Her dark tent—

One ink-stained sheet: hyacinthine
canvas—rough-cut
from a hired demon's song,
windproof and waterproof
pounding board. Made from rags,
wood and grasses, this biblical structure,
cut 8 by 10, to invent on
and curse on, ride out the storm,
to resurrect again and again.
Admix of wonder and that which
inspires dread. Here the roof truss
at the straining beam incarnate.
World-shaped bowery: a blue-bag
prophesied through a God's eye.

Sylvia's Color Chart

She follows an owl's ghost
over a Charles River bridge,
a bag of steaks and bottle
of golden sherry in one hand,
in the other a book on the Church's
views of Physical Love in Marriage.
That season, though, sex:
a hue, palette, tone, timbre.

Paper Dolls: Midnight Blue Gown with Cape

Gown sculpted from night sky, stitched with Eve's tears. Stars spin around the skin-tight blue tent. She is ready for anything blue now. Midnight blue cape. Midnight ocean. A bodice-wrapped full-moon reflection, moonskin across a low tide. A gown lined with two magenta waves: wave and inner wave solidified for a viola lesson or an evening of rabbiting. Hunting fish-glass in a gown of cave-glow. Curvy, up against blue French doors. French doors always just barely ajar. She strokes a blue kitten, gazes out at a man in black on the magenta breakwater. *Venus, anti-Venus, Venus, anti-Venus* she counts on the petals of an upside-down flower. Curvy blue, she plucks a pair of children's scissors hanging from a tree and cuts five yellow stars out of the sky. She places one star on her hip, one between her breasts, one on each slipper, and one on her matching midnight blue mask. The great Connemara sky cows' butter, the sugar-and-butter stars.

Things to Eat, Paris, 1953

White beans, brandy, escargot, cake,
cognac, steak tartare, sardines,
coffee in bed every morning,
onion soup, wine, a club sandwich,
orange pressé, sardines, herring,
oysters, Cinzano, coq au vin,
nuts, fruit, red wine, cold fish.
She took a borrowed Olivetti to Paris
and read about wild beasts. She wanted
to marry a big man. Soon she would meet
Ted Hughes and bite him until he bled
after several cocktails. Ted believed
he was possessed by a ghost-wolf
that wanted to be a real wolf, a devourer.
Assia said he smelled like a butcher in bed.

Wedding Invitation III

Mr. and Mrs. Naked and Bald
have the Wind's Sneer of announcing
the Opaque Belly-scale
of their daughter
Dark Flesh, Dark Pairings
to
Easter Egg, the Ill-starred Thing
on Sunday, the Brute, Brute of September
The Suck of the Sea, New Jersey

Sylvia's Laughter

Held in the back of the rare books library
in a box marked *Poet's Laughter, 1955-1963,*
I open folio O, and discover an explosion

of vowel-based notes severed from gut and lung-sac,
the product of 15 facial muscles, preserved, contracted,
bought discount at an auction from a dealer in sentiment.

My God what a laugh! Belts, girdles, garters—
a siren suit and dog dish. Oh I feel the laugh inside
—full of sex—and something else

rare and extinct like rubbing your hands
across a running lynx. In the past power
in a closed smile, a closed mouth. No teeth.

All dreams are filed jokes, says the doctor.
An envelope and label for each snicker and giggle.
The Christ child stands alone, sucks an adding machine,

spasms glass. Ted's dirty crow. Mermaid tits.
How many lightbulbs does it take to turn a girl
into a tree and back again? O hilarious roots.

Bought at a price, in accordance with the established
principles of excellence in Arts and Sciences.
Money smiles, smells the suspect's fingers.

Wedding Invitation IV

Mr. and Mrs. Free Fish-Bait
insist on the Fixed Vortex of your Spidery Wazzle-dazzle
at the Brilliant Cutlery of their Small Island
Amnesias of Heaven
to
Mr. My Fear, My Fear, My Fear
on Saturday, the Trump-crack of Edwardian Sentiments
nineteen hundred of Mouth-plugs
at God-ball
The Bottle in Which I Live, Massachusetts

Paper Dolls: Yellow Lightbulb Party Dress

Yellow lightbulb dress for an evening dance on the Saranac. As if firefly light were a fabric. To dance in a church without a roof among elongated shadows and spilled stars, shy, freckles unfurled, threads and other sewing matter, the ancient and aromatic ferns. Champagne of musical motifs, bubbly, flowing, free-form except for the tight belt at the waist. She is encased in shellac. A cage of secrets. At the neck, a black thread to be plugged in. Let's tap-dance in time to the on-off switch. Her legs together, one knee slightly bent. Transparent yolk and transparent trim. Four buttons. Pushed-up breasts. A circuitry of liquid—gauzy cords of six imaginary ingredients. World host to many worlds. This madness called love.

Sylvia's Hair

A handkerchief box, a perfume of the day, four pieces of yellowed tape. Five locks of hair, one braid, a safety pin, drawing paper, folded brown flowers. Cream envelopes, sticky glue, hair peeking out over the top.

Silken hair from seed pods drifts through trees, wisps blow along the moist coast, balled-up hair found under a mattress.

At the age of twelve years and ten months Sylvia Plath's braids were cut.

Horsetails. Still full of gold, phallic, strings of utterance—

The tongue of the world, the mouth-starved world, clock teeth wrapped in hair, empty wax paper, folded for lunch or after. *Jesus hair.*

She is in the basement. A little blue bow. Soft swirl of underarm hair, downy duck feathers on the inside of the thigh...*bean flowers...*

Sweetly, sweetly she breathes, how soft the night glow—

She says: I'll tell you two secrets, come close, very close:

I am murdered.
I did not kill myself.

See how the world cuts and eats us plain and fancy.

There's another lock of hair tucked inside an envelope labeled *extra buttons.*

A plain gingham tablecloth, a picnic basket of jams and berries, a prickly wind blowing seagrass and seaweed slightly to the south—crackling blue light, so much light, nodding and rocking and fingering her thin hair—fingers red from berries. The silver edge of the scissor's blade when the cut takes place.

Acknowledgments and Notes

These inklings, riffs, and big-picture imaginings celebrate, investigate, and improvise on the life and work of Sylvia Plath. They are based on her published and unpublished work, as well as hearsay and real-life events. Several poems in the collection came out of my meanderings through the Sylvia Plath materials housed in the Lilly Library, the rare books, manuscripts, and special collections library at Indiana University, Bloomington. I spent many a pleasurable and snowy afternoon with the Plath materials, looking at the drafts, letters, photographs, and memorabilia. It is difficult to express the tenderness evoked by spending time with this repository of feelings, this locked cabinet of things that Plath touched or created—a tenderness that softens the dominant vision of Plath as an icon frozen in time, reduced to a definitive set of contours—tragic, brilliant, fully and finally processed. This book was a way for me to get to know Sylvia Plath, and I am deeply grateful for the opportunity. The textures revealed by the archive, the life revealed by and embodied in these objects—the diary, her braid, her instructions to her children's nanny, her paper dolls, her passport, her marginalia, her own artwork—offer, I hope, another way to go back to Plath as well as to go forward: an unofficial biography, an unofficial life.

"Sylvia's Mouths" is a collage of phrases using the word "mouth" from poems by Sylvia Plath.

"Viola Practice, 1945," "Eternal Blackout," Sylvia's Sled," "Paradise, 1956," "Sylvia's Snakecharmer," "Last Wishes, 1963," "Stars that year—," "Things to Do, 1944," "Diary Starts, 1943," "Things to Eat, Paris, 1955," "Things to Do, 1951," "Summer Dates," "Sylvia's Ritual," "Things to Do, 1953," and "Sylvia's Color Chart" are derived from and inspired by the Plath materials at the Lilly Library, especially the childhood diaries, clippings, daily journals, and calendars, 1944-1957; a record of summer dates, 1949; the Ted Hughes manuscripts, 1957-1960; the Plath manuscripts, collection III, 1941-1951, consisting of

Plath's drawings, paintings, pastel works, and college art projects by Sylvia Plath; her Baby Book, circa 1932-1933; high school memorabilia; art scrapbooks relating to design, color, and arrangement; papers, tests, and assignments; *Mademoiselle* materials relating to College Board and guest editorship; letters and cards from Plath to Gordon Ames Lameyer; and check stubs relating to publications.

The wedding-invitation poems are based on 22 invitations Plath received from 1953 through 1955, purchased by the Lilly Library. The names, dates, and locations are replaced with small fragments from poems by Plath.

The paper-doll poems are based on the 118 paper dolls and costumes handmade by Plath, 57 purchased paper dolls and costumes, and one envelope with five decals at the Lilly Library.

"Sylvia's Hair" and "Sylvia's Snakecharmer" are based on samples of Plath's hair (including one lock, 1932; one lock, 1938; one lock, July 30, 1941; a tress, August 1942; braids, August 22, 1945; and one lock, fall 1949) housed at the Lilly Library.

"Sylvia's Passport" is based on Sylvia's Plath's passport, 1955, also housed at the Lilly Library.

"Irresistible blaze" is a quote form Robert Lowell's introduction to *Ariel* by Sylvia Plath

Thanks and acknowledgment go to the following publications, where these poems previously appeared, sometimes in different versions: *Conjunctions, Court Green, Sonora Review,* and *TriQuarterly.*

I wish to thank my friend Barbara J. Orton for her extraordinarily keen ears and eyes and all her help reading drafts of the poems along the way. For her support and wise counsel, I am ever grateful to Four Way Books editor, the elegantly enthusiastic and sharp-witted Sally Ball. I'm also grateful to Plath scholar and organizer-visionary Kathleen Connors for inviting me to write a poem for the Sylvia Plath 70th Year Commemoration Concert at Indiana University's Jacob School of Music and for the Sylvia Plath 75th Year Symposium in Oxford—an invitation that planted the seeds for this collection—and for offering so much biographical insight and expertise. Thanks also to Martha Rhodes for her commitment. My thanks and appreciation for the unwearied assistance offered by Becky Cape, Sue Presnell, and Michael Taylor of the Lilly Library. I'm grateful to my mother, Tita Bowman. And thanks also to Alita Hornick, Susan Gubar, Laughing Womyn Ashonosheni, Kristen Nash, and Maura Saunton. Thanks to Indiana University and the Corporation of Yaddo for their support. And much love and many thanks to Mark Harrison.

Catherine Bowman was born in El Paso, Texas. Her previous collections are *1-800-HOT-RIBS, Rock Farm,* and *Notarikon*. She is the editor of *Word of Mouth: Poems Featured on NPR's* All Things Considered. She lives in Bloomington, Indiana, and teaches in the creative writing program at Indiana University.